THE GALAPAGOS MURDER

THE MURDER MYSTERY THAT ROCKED
THE EQUATOR

COLD CASE CRIME SERIES #5

FERGUS MASON

Absolute Crime Press
ANAHEIM, CALIFORNIA

ABSO UTE CR ME

www.AbsoluteCrime.com

Contents

ABOUT ABSOLUTE CRIME

Absolute Crime publishes only the best true crime literature. Our focus is on the crimes that you've probably never heard of, but you are fascinated to read more about. With each engaging and gripping story, we try to let readers relive moments in history that some people have tried to forget.

Remember, our books are not meant for the faint at heart. We don't hold back--if a crime is bloody, we let the words splatter across the page so you can experience the crime in the most horrifying way!

If you enjoy this book, please visit our homepage (www.AbsoluteCrime.com) to see other books we offer; if you have any feedback, we'd love to hear from you!

Sign up for our mailing list, and we'll send you out a free true crime book!

http://www.absolutecrime.com/newsletter

INTRODUCTION

Despite a decline in the number of murders in the United States since the 1960s, thousands go unsolved each year. As of 2013, the solve rate was at an all time low at only 65 percent of the total committed. The following 15 murders were committed

between 1958 and 2014. The oldest of the set involves the bizarre murder of Pearl Eaton, one of the famous Ziegfeld Follies Girls of the 1920s.

The Galápagos Islands lie right on the Equator in the South Pacific Ocean, about six hundred miles off the coast of Ecuador, and nobody's quite sure how long they've been there. The islands have been studied more by biologists than geologists and the most we know is that they're volcanic, created – like Hawaii – by a "hot spot" under the Earth's crust, and that as an island group they're somewhere between 8 million and 90 million years old. The hot spot is still active and the two newest islands, Isabella and Fernandina, continue to grow as fresh lava periodically surges up from the depths of the Earth. These islands are right over the hot spot itself; the ones to their east are older, carried away from the subterranean fire by the slow movement of the Nazca Plate as it slides under South America. On the seabed a trail of even older islands, eroded away until their highest points are far below the surface, straggles towards a deep trench just off the Ecuadorean coast. The Galápagos hot spot has been creating islands for at least half a billion years and, eventually, they all reach the coast and get carried back down into the molten depths.

Floreana won't be disappearing for a while. One of the smaller of the main islands, and further south than any but Española, it's no longer volcanically active but probably was in the fairly recent past. Eleven miles long and nine wide, it's mostly flat but in the center rises to the 2,100 foot peak of Cerro Pajas, the old volcano that formed the island long ago.

Volcanic rock breaks down into rich soil and despite their isolation the Galápagos Islands support a lot of life. Long ago they were colonized by iguanas, tortoises, rodents and various birds. Living in small numbers on separate islands these species, and the native plants, have gradually evolved into unique forms. Most tortoises are small but the Galápagos Tortoise is the size of a small sofa and weights up to 900 pounds; each subspecies lives on only one island. Iguanas are found throughout Mexico, Central America and the Caribbean, and along with other lizards have made it to the Galápagos too. There's another type of iguana on the islands though – the world's only marine lizard. It's found on all the Galápagos islands and nowhere else in the world. The birds are unusual too. Darwin's Finches – which aren't really finches at all – are also unique to the islands, as is the Flightless Cormorant.

It's unknown when people first discovered the islands. Pottery fragments and other debris suggest native South American peoples had visited there, but the earliest sighting by Europeans was on March 10, 1535, when a lost

Spanish ship carrying the Bishop of Panama landed there. By 1570 they were being marked on maps as "Insulae de los Galopegos," the Islands of the Tortoises. English explorer and occasional pirate Richard Hawkins visited in 1593. More English pirates arrived in the late 17th century, using the islands as a base for their raids on Spanish treasure galleons carrying gold and silver down the coast; the buccaneers haunted the Galápagos until the middle of the 18th century. By then whalers were also using the islands, filling their water casks there and stocking up on meat. The pirates had released goats on the islands and they bred rapidly, creating a food resource for the sea raiders, but the whaling ships preferred to capture the giant tortoises. The lumbering reptiles could survive for months without food or water; ships could keep hundreds of them alive in the hold, slaughtering them when meat was needed. As the Pacific whaling industry grew tortoise numbers plummeted and several subspecies were completely wiped out. Fur traders also pillaged the islands, decimating the seal population. More invasive species arrived too; the Spanish

Viceroy of Peru, hoping to wipe out the goats the pirates ate, unleashed feral dogs on the islands and later sailors released cattle and pigs. Cats and rats came ashore from the ships, and foreign plant species were introduced. All this had a serious effect on the island ecosystems; the cattle and goats ate the vegetation the tortoises relied on, while cats, dogs and pigs raided their nests. Nobody knows exactly how many species became extinct.

Floreana suffered more than most. On October 22 1819 a crewman from the American whaling ship Essex started a fire as a prank; unfortunately it was the middle of the dry season and it spread out of control, devastating most of the island.1 A group of tortoise hunters from the Essex were trapped and had to run through the fire to escape, and the captain was furious. Threatening dire punishments if he ever caught the culprit he ordered the Essex back to sea and she sailed out towards the catching grounds in the southern Pacific. A year later – whalers routinely made two or three year voyages – she launched her whaleboats to pursue a pod of sperm whales 2,000 miles west of the

Galápagos. Suddenly a large whale broke away from the boats, headed straight for the ship and slammed his forehead into her hull.2 The Essex sank in ten minutes and the twenty men on board had to escape in the whaleboats. In the end twelve died; several were eaten by their starving shipmates. In 1841 Herman Melville, on his first voyage on the whaler Acushnet, heard the tale and was inspired to write Moby Dick.

The fire didn't wipe out all life on Floreana, because several whalers reported collecting tortoises there over the next few years. It did cause immense damage though because when Thomas Nickerson, the former cabin boy of the Essex, returned there years later the island was still a wasteland of ash. The vegetation recovered slowly and several unique animal species probably disappeared in the fire.

In September 1835 a small British warship, the 10-gun sloop HMS Beagle, arrived in the Galápagos and began a five-week exploration of the islands. Many Royal Navy sailors thought HMS Beagle was an unlucky ship; within weeks of being launched in 1820 she had been declared redundant and left to rot at anchor for five years. Refitted as a survey ship she sailed to South America in May 1826 for a four-year voyage, which was interrupted in 1828 when her captain became depressed and shot himself. By the time the ship reached Montevideo she needed urgent repairs, after which she resumed her mission under a new captain, Lieutenant Robert FitzRoy. Off the coast of Tierra del Fuego a group of locals stole one of the ship's boats and FitzRoy took four of them hostage as a reprisal, then brought them back to England. In 1831 the disintegrating ship was fully rebuilt and modified to make her less dangerous in bad weather, then sailed for South America again in December that year. FitzRoy was worried though. The captain of a warship lived a stressful life and, even in a vessel as cramped as the Beagle (she was only 90 feet long and 24 feet wide) was very isolated from the junior officers and crew. Captain Stokes, his predecessor, had killed himself after cracking under the strain and FitzRoy's uncle had cut his own throat in 1822;3 the young captain was

convinced that he was at risk of suicide too.1
To reduce the risk he decided to take a "gentleman companion," who unlike the crew it would be acceptable for him to socialize with. There was also the chance of killing two birds with one stone here – on his first voyage he'd been frustrated by the lack of a geologist in the crew, and if he could find one to come with him it would help with the surveying as well as his own sanity. After a couple of false starts he did, although the young man he found was usually seasick and spent as little time as possible on board the ship; he preferred to ride overland between ports, rejoining the Beagle whenever she anchored. In between he chased wildlife, studied the land, nearly killed himself trying to throw a bolas and helped put down an armed rebellion. He couldn't ride to the Galápagos though; he had to sail there. So when FitzRoy landed on Floreana on September 23, 1835 he brought with him, rather green and glad to be back on dry land, Charles Darwin.

---

[1] He was. In 1865, after being refused a promotion, he followed his uncle's example and cut his own throat with a razor.

We think of Darwin as a stooped old man, weakened by years of illness and almost hidden behind a bushy white beard. When he visited the Galápagos he was only 26, though, and he was tall, powerful and energetic. He'd already been on several of the islands and seen the tortoises there, and he busily searched for more on Floreana. It's often claimed that all he found was empty shells. In fact Darwin reported that there was a penal colony of two to three hundred Ecuadorean political prisoners on the island and, although there were plenty of wild goats and pigs in the regrown forests, most of the meat they ate came from tortoises.4 While on Floreana – which he called by its English name of Charles Island – he also met the islands' vice governor; Nicholas Lawson – Norwegian by birth, British by choice and naturalization, and now working for the government of Ecuador – had been on Floreana to inspect a whaling ship, and now he spent some time with Darwin. The islands and the small penal colony didn't need much government so Lawson had a lot of spare time, and he'd spent much of it learning about the wildlife. The tortoises were different on each island, he explained; show him a tortoise – even the shell – and he could tell you right away what island it came from. Darwin was mainly a geologist at the time and only dabbled in biology, but what Lawson was saying interested him because he'd noticed that each island also had its own species of mockingbird. He was too busy exploring to think much about that at the time, but 24 years later he published a book that caused a bit of excitement for a while.

The convicts Darwin saw had been on Floreana since Ecuador claimed the islands in 1832 (and had eaten all the island's tortoises by 1850) and they were the first attempt at setting up a permanent colony on the Galápagos. It wasn't a success, but the Ecuadoreans kept trying. Other settlers came and went over the decades, but few stayed long (except the convicts, who didn't get to choose). In 1925 a group of 22 Norwegians arrived; four years later only two remained, running a fishing boat together with an Ecuadorean settler.5 In June 1929 they left too, admitting defeat after their fishing sloop was blown 30 miles north to another island, Santa Cruz, in a storm. Floreana was left deserted once more – but not for long.

In September 1929 two new settlers arrived on the desolate island. A bizarre couple, more visitors would soon be drawn by the ideals they promoted. Minor fame finally came to Floreana – and in its wake, mystery and tragedy.

NOTES

[1] Nickerson, Thomas; *Account of the Ship* Essex *Sinking, 1819-1821*
http://www.galapagos.to/TEXTS/NICKERSON.HTM

[2] Faiella, Graham; *Moby Dick and the Whaling Industry of the 19th Century*, p. 27

[3] Pratchett, Terry; Cohen, Ian; Stewart, Jack; *The Science of Discworld III – Darwin's Watch* pp. 120-121

[4] Darwin, Charles; *The Voyage of the Beagle*, p. 357

[5] Treherne, John; *The Galapagos Affair*

CHAPTER 1

Friedrich Ritter was born in Wollbach, in Germany's Black Forest region, on May 24, 1886. The Black Forest is very different from the exposed equatorial island of Floreana. Nearly 250 miles from the nearest coast, it's an area of rolling hills, sandstone cliffs and dark, brooding pine forests, scattered with pocket size fields and tiny villages. Officially part of the small town of Kandern, Wollbach is a collection of a few dozen houses and three old mills two and a half miles to the south. In winter the surrounding hills mean the sun rises late and sets early, and in late December there's barely eight hours of daylight. The houses have steeply pitched roofs to shed heavy snow. Friedrich grew up in the strict, conservative society of a German village where beatings at home and school were part of life, hard work was expected and the surrounding forests seem to swallow both sound and light. He was a weak boy, often unwell, and in many ways it was a miserable life for him. He spent his free time wandering in the forests, developing a love of the silent woods and the animals that lived there.1

Although sickly Friedrich was both a keen reader and good with his hands; his father, who worked as a carpenter as well as running a village store, taught him how to work with wood. He had mechanical aptitude too. Once, when his mother was out, he dismantled her sewing machine – which fascinated him – and reassembled it. Later in his life he liked to tell people how it had worked better after he rebuilt it. When he wasn't studying or learning practical skills he enjoyed reading, especially adventure stories. Among his favorites were Daniel Defoe's Robinson Crusoe and the frontier novels of J. Fenimore Cooper. His intelligence was obvious, and after leaving school he applied for a place at the university in Freiburg, twenty miles to the north. He was accepted, and moved into a student lodging house to begin his studies.

Modern Germany is famous for its scientific achievements and superb engineering, but that's a recent thing. From the fall of the Roman Empire until the rise of Prussian dominance in the 19th century, which became complete with the establishment of the German Empire under Otto Von Bismarck in 1871, Germany was a patchwork of small states and had a reputation in Europe for being socially and technologically backwards. A swarm of minor princes and dukes ruled the tiny countries and wasted their resources building palaces and squabbling with each other. Some cities objected to this and managed to break free, so the unhappy land was studded with an assortment of free cities; these tended to thrive. Hamburg, for example, was the heart of the Hanseatic League, a trading network of free cities that dominated commerce from Calais to the Baltic, and along the river Rhine, for over 400 years. Nuremberg was an art center that played a huge part in the Renaissance in northern Europe. Freiburg chose a different route to influence; it became a center of advanced education.

Freiburg im Breisgau was founded as a free city in 1120 and quickly became rich from the production of nearby silver mines. The university was established in 1457, making it the fifth oldest in Germany, and quickly became a real rival to the top European colleges of the time. Today it's rated sixth in Europe in terms of its impact on science, putting it in a small elite headed by Oxford and Cambridge. In the Middle Ages it became a home for free thinkers, despite occasional persecution by the religious authorities, and that had an influence on Freiburg itself. As the influence of the Jesuits was suppressed in the 18th century it increasingly became a place where radical ideas were tolerated, and even encouraged. When Friedrich Ritter arrived there in 1904 it was a huge change from the conservative village where he had grown up. Now he was mixing with philosophers, political reformers, alternative medicine advocates and early environmentalists, all living a Bohemian lifestyle. In 1900 Freiburg had become the first German university to admit female students and was seen as socially very liberal.

The social attitudes of the university spilled over into the city itself and things that would have been unacceptable in the rigid society of southwest Germany were just fine in Freiburg. Friedrich found himself sharing an apartment with a young music student, Mila Clark. It wasn't long before they started a relationship and in 1906, aged 20, Friedrich married her. His family was furious but Friedrich ignored them; he was still studying – chemistry, physics and philosophy, then medicine – but he also took an interest in his new wife's career, which was fairly successful; she found a place with the Royal Opera in Darmstadt and sang several major parts there. Promoting Mila slowed his progress towards a medical degree (which is slow anyway in Germany – it's not uncommon for qualifying as a doctor to take well over a decade) and he still hadn't graduated when the First World War began in 1914. Early in the war he volunteered for the German Army and spent four years as an artillery officer, then returned to Freiburg to complete his studies. The city had been close to the southern end of the Western Front and had suffered from air attacks more than once, but it had also served as a medical center for wounded troops;2 that had spurred rapid progress at the medical school, and even as Germany fell apart in the revolutionary turmoil that followed the war some of the best medical training in the world was available there.

After graduating Friedrich started looking for a job as a doctor, and found a place at the University of Berlin's Hydrotherapeutic Institute. Hydrotherapy, the use of water in healing, has been practiced since ancient times; some of the best historical examples are the Roman baths. It's been widespread in Germany since the 1840s, a time when it went through a major revival in the USA and most of Europe, and remains popular today – Germany has many health resorts with hydrotherapy clinics or natural hot baths, and their health insurance system can (and often does) prescribe up to six weeks in a spa. In fact Germans like all sorts of traditional and alternative medicines, and working in hydrotherapy in a major university was a prestigious job. Friedrich's career was off to a good start.

His marriage, on the other hand, wasn't. Mila Ritter was a lot more conventional than her husband and expected that, now that she was married, she should give up singing professionally and become a full time Hausfrau. Friedrich disagreed; Mila's talent was a large part of what had attracted him to her and he had ambitions for her career. Much more forceful and determined than Mila, he refused to let her stop working to keep house for him. The relationship quickly became strained, so when Friedrich developed an attraction for a female patient he was willing to act on it.

Dore Strauch was married to a schoolteacher 22 years older than her, and it wasn't working out well. She was attracted to art and philosophy, and supported the ideals of the leftist revolution that had erupted in Germany after the war.3 By 1926 she was in a highly conventional marriage and was looking for some excitement in her life. She was also looking for treatment for the multiple sclerosis that was making her life a misery, and her family doctor had recommended hydrotherapy.

When she arrived at the Institute for Hydrotherapy Dore was at first alarmed by an intense, overbearing young doctor; she hoped, she later wrote, that he wouldn't be treating her. However she soon changed her mind when he began discussing philosophy with her, especially the works of Friedrich Nietzsche.4 She was also receptive to his ideas about the healing power of the mind – he told her that even multiple sclerosis would respond to the power of positive thinking. By the time she was discharged two weeks later the pair were firm friends, and she agreed to the doctor's suggestion that he become her personal physician. The domineering young doctor was Friedrich Ritter.

It wasn't long before Ritter and Strauch began an affair. She'd already told him how unhappy she was with her marriage, and his own was falling apart too. Frustrated with their spouses, they spent time together in the rooms above Ritter's private practice in Kalckreuthstrasse. Located just south of the Tiergarten, the huge park that makes up Berlin's green heart, Ritter's clinic was in a five-story apartment block with a large flat roof. The couple would climb up there and lie on the tiles, watching the clouds and talking philosophy. Gradually they decided to leave Germany behind them and build themselves a paradise based on Nietzsche's ideals. At some point the decision was made that they would settle on the Galápagos Islands. It made sense – since the 1920s the Ecuadorean government had been trying to attract settlers to the islands, and they were offering free plots of land with hunting and fishing rights and a ten-year tax holiday.5

Of course there were some loose ends to be tidied up first. Both Ritter and Strauch had inconvenient spouses and they applied some ingenuity to the question of how to get them out the way. Their solution was at the same time remarkably neat and utterly unbelievable – persuade the abandoned wife and husband to move in with each other and let the couple leave. What's even more unbelievable is that Mila Ritter and Dr. Körwin agreed to the scheme. With the biggest obstacle out of the way Ritter began collecting the supplies they'd need to establish themselves on a tropical island. Tools, reference books and household items were stockpiled – everything they thought they would need. Or at least, almost everything. Ritter wanted to take a rifle; Strauch vetoed it because it didn't fit in with the ideal of living in harmony with nature. Strauch wanted to take drugs and medical supplies. Ritter refused…because it didn't fit in with the ideal of living in harmony with nature.

There might have been gaps in their inventory, but Ritter and Strauch were happy with it. By June 1929 they were making the final preparations – arranging transport for themselves and their belongings. Last letters were written to family and friends, surplus belongings were disposed of and they packed their stockpile. Some of their preparations were more bizarre. Ritter was worried about the lack of dental facilities on the island so he had all his teeth extracted; he planned to chew using his gums but packed a set of stainless steel dentures for emergencies. Some sources say that Strauch also had her teeth extracted and the dentures were shared,6 but this is an urban legend.

Finally they were ready. Their boxes were loaded on a train to Amsterdam, and on July 3, 1929 they set sail on the SS Boskoop.7

The Boskoop was a Dutch freighter that was also fitted out to carry up to 88 passengers. She was a new ship, launched in Rotterdam only two years earlier, and with nearly as many crew as passengers it was a comfortable trip. The reality of what they were doing started to hit home in early August when, after passing through the Panama Canal, they landed in Ecuador. It was a chance to add a few last minute purchases to their collection of gear, but that wouldn't take long and they'd learned that the ship to their final destination on Floreana wouldn't be sailing until the end of the month. That gave them plenty of time to do some sightseeing – and what they saw was a shock. Shrunken heads displayed in a church were barbaric but exotic. The harsh terrain was an unwelcome surprise to both Germans, though, and the poverty and squalor was like nothing they'd ever seen. Strauch, who was partly disabled because of her multiple sclerosis, suffered badly in the thin mountain air when they visited

Quito, which is over 9,000 feet above sea level. She survived, however, and on August 31 the pair boarded the ship for the final leg to the Galápagos.

The Manuel y Cobos couldn't have been more different from the SS Boskoop. The Dutch ship was a modern, well-equipped steam freighter; the Cobos was an ancient sailing vessel, a coastal schooner that had seen better days. Her rotting hull was badly trimmed, dragged down at the stern by the weight of an engine she'd never been designed to carry. The decks were splattered with dung from her last cargo of cows.8 Ritter had booked a first-class cabin, which turned out to be a tiny cubbyhole that stank of engine exhaust. There were four of these cabins on board, but sixty passengers (and another hundred cattle.) Most of the passengers slept wherever they could, scattered among the ship's gear.

The schooner moored briefly off Floreana early in September; Ritter unloaded most of his supplies and the ship's captain, a colorful Norwegian named Bruuns, left a teenage Indian named Hugo to watch the crates – and carry out one of his own business schemes. Bruuns supplemented his income from shipping by hunting the wild cattle that lived on Floreana, selling their hides and salted beef on the mainland. While Ritter and Strauch toured the rest of the Galápagos on the ship Hugo would shoot as many of the scrawny animals as he could with his old-fashioned musket.

The two Germans returned to Floreana on September 19. Right away Strauch began to have doubts about her new home. She could see small fish swimming in the clear water around the ship but further out there were large, ominous forms visible beneath the surface.9 She was right to be worried. There's a species of shark named for the islands – the Galápagos Shark – but it's fairly harmless. It's not alone though. Two of the three shark species responsible for most attributed attacks on humans are often found around the Galápagos; the Great White and the Tiger shark, known as "the dustbin of the sea" for its voracious and indiscriminate appetite. They might not even be the worst danger. French naturalist Jacques Cousteau always claimed that the Oceanic

White Tip is "the most dangerous of all sharks,"10 even though it's officially blamed for quite a small number of deaths. Most of the White Tip's victims are killed and eaten in the open ocean, so no trace is ever found. They're a serious danger to survivors of shipwrecks and air disasters. When the USS Indianapolis was torpedoed in the Pacific in 1945 White Tips killed up to 80 of the 880 men who escaped from the sinking ship. Normally they're not a hazard to swimmers because they stay in deep water far from the coast, but in the Galápagos Islands the steep slopes of the submerged volcanoes mean they're often found close to the shore.

There were hazards on land, too. Ritter, Strauch and Hugo – who had agreed to stay for a while to help them settle in - spent their first night in the house built by the previous Norwegian settlers. In September temperatures on Floreana usually fall to below 50°F at night, which is cold enough to make sleeping in the open unattractive. Next day they stored their supplies of food and seeds in the abandoned Norwegian buildings to keep them safe from animals, packed three days' worth of supplies in their rucksacks and set out to explore the island. Their first priority was to find a spot to build their new home.

At this point it's tempting to wonder why they didn't simply move into the abandoned house built by the Norwegians. It was a two-floor structure built from timber and corrugated iron, and would have suited them well. The Norwegians had also constructed outbuildings, a blacksmith's forge, a pier and a narrow gauge railway for moving supplies from the beach to the house.11 It was also in an ideal location, at a natural harbor where ships had been anchoring for centuries. Over a hundred years before the crew of a whaler had driven a post deep into the beach and mounted a small wooden barrel on it. Sailors from visiting ships would leave letters in the barrel, new arrivals would check its contents and, if any of the letters were addressed near their destination, they'd take them with them. It was a trust-based unofficial postal system that works well – and continues to; the barrel is still standing –

and it gained the anchorage the name of Post Office Bay.

The problem with the house was that it was too good. Ritter dreamed of a Robinson Crusoe-style existence, using their initial batch of supplies to get established then producing everything they needed for themselves. There was no place in his scheme for a ready-built house; they would have to build their own. Now they set off into the island's interior to look for a location. Again that's a decision that just made things harder for them, because any supplies they received would need to come in by sea and the further from the coast they lived, the further they'd have to carry everything. Ritter was adamant though, so off they went.

It soon became obvious that the terrain was a lot rougher than they'd expected. The volcanic rock of the island had often splintered as it cooled, and the result was patches littered with lethally sharp blades that cut their feet, even through their heavy walking shoes. The heat was also crippling and they were both suffering badly by the time they stopped for the night. They slept in a cave high on the mountain – they believed it had been enlarged by an Irish pirate, and at first Hugo was frightened to sleep in it in case the buccaneer's ghost returned – and resumed their search next day. Finally, on the third day, they found the perfect place – a bowl-shaped crater on the slopes of the mountain. The soil on the floor of the extinct vent was rich and deep, and it was overgrown with vegetation; a natural spring in the middle fed a small stream.12 Ritter named the spot Friedo, a contraction of Friedrich and Dore.

The chosen location was beautiful and had outstanding views of the ocean, but it was 500 feet above sea level and it wasn't easy to get their gear up to it. They captured a wild horse but Ritter soon managed to work it to death. In October a visiting ship left them a stronger horse, which let them carry their heavier baggage up the hill. The supplies Ritter had packed included rolls of roofing felt and bales of cloth; how he had expected to move them without pack animals is a mystery.

Among the supplies were large quantities of seeds and plant cuttings and they planted a garden in the crater soon after settling there. Their first crops grew with amazing speed, as did the house now taking shape there. The house was another challenge. Ritter had decided that the best building material was acacia wood, despite the acacia tree almost never growing straight. To make use of the curved trunks he built an oval house covered in roofing felt to keep the rain out. Later the ship that had given them the horse donated a stack of corrugated iron that Ritter used to build a weather-resistant roof. It was a strange house, and after the rainy season it became even stranger – the unseasoned and still-living acacia of the walls sprouted leaves.

Unfortunately the hard work of setting up home on the island had brought out the more unpleasant side of Ritter's personality, and he had become cruel and dismissive to Strauch. The reality of living in a tropical paradise was a long way from the dreams they'd shared lying on a rooftop in Berlin. Strauch was now having serious doubts about the relationship but she was determined to make a success of the project. Despite health problems she struggled on, working in the garden and around the house. Gradually things got better. The garden never repeated the spectacular success of the first growing season but did give them a steady supply of food. Exotic fruit grew wild on the island. After Hugo left with Captain Bruun they settled down to a life of vegetarianism and nudism, closely in line with Ritter's philosophical ideals.

Within months there were signs of problems on the horizon, though. Yachts frequently visited the Galápagos, and many of the visitors met the couple. On returning home the yachtsmen talked about their experiences and the story of the eccentric German naturists began to spread. Newspapers picked up on it, and various versions of the story generated interest. Some of them were wildly inaccurate – the tale of the shared dentures is a perfect example. An increasing number of people felt inspired by the romantic idea of voluntary castaways, and some of them actually made the long trip to the Galápagos to visit them.

The couple seemed conflicted about these visitors; Ritter resented them while Strauch tried her best to make them feel welcome.13 Some of them wanted to stay – a group of young Germans settled in the caves on the mountain, while one eccentric German woman tried to persuade Ritter to let her move in to Friedo, then moved on to the Norwegian house in Post Office Bay. This house was now occupied again, by Captain Bruuns, who had restarted his countrymen's abandoned fishing operation. It was no tropical paradise though, but a hardworking business outpost staffed by ten Indians and reeking of fish guts. Offal and blood from the processed catch were dumped in the bay, which had become a seething pool of ravenous sharks. Strauch hated the place and it seems the strange female visitor felt the same, because she only stayed a week before sailing back to Ecuador.

CHAPTER 2

Most of the visitors were Germans, because
the German press covered the couple more
frequently and because naturist philosophy had
a strong appeal in the country. In 1931 another
family arrived to settle; former infantry officer
Heinz Wittmer, his pregnant wife Margret and
twelve-year-old Harry, Heinz's son from his first
marriage, who was going blind. Heinz had been
severely traumatized by his service in the
trenches, facing gas attacks and squalor for
four years – not what he'd expected when he'd
joined the reserves before the war. After Germany's collapse he struggled to find work in
the disintegrating economy. For a while he
worked in the office of Konrad Adenauer, who
at that time was the mayor of Cologne14 but
later became the first leader of West Germany.
Finally he'd had enough and, inspired by

stories of the pioneering couple on the Galápagos, decided to join them.

The Wittmers shared Ritter and Strauch's dream of self-sufficiency on a tropical island, but seemed more practical; among other things they brought firearms with them and were prepared to hunt to supplement their diets. The Wittmers had reached Floreana after a three-week stop on Chatham Island and they were exhausted. They quickly set about establishing themselves though. Ritter and Strauch suggested they use the caves – now deserted by the young Germans – as a temporary home, and although it was a struggle they managed to haul their belongings up the slope. They also quickly began clearing and planting a garden. As Strauch had found, the feral livestock on the island was a serious menace to crops; pigs and wild bulls determinedly broke through any fences to trample and eat the plants. Ritter had driven himself half mad trying to trap one boar, culminating in a dynamite booby trap that risked demolishing their house. When bulls started launching similar attacks on the

Wittmer's garden the practical Heinz simply loaded his old Mauser service rifle and shot them.15

Once they'd moved all their gear into the hills the Wittmers began building a temporary home, a log cabin on a foundation of lava stones. Ritter and Strauch were also planning a new house to replace their acacia structure, which was beginning to warp and splinter as the climate distorted the wood. Ritter told visitors about his great plans involving a grand building of quarried stone, but the task defeated him and the new dwelling at Freido ended up as a crude metal roof supported on posts, with canvas screens that could be rolled down to close the sides. In the center was a small cage of wire mesh where the pair slept, in an attempt to fend off the ants that constantly invaded. Meanwhile Heinz and Margret completed their sensible, practical hut and started working leisurely on their permanent home. Ritter sneered at Heinz Wittmer's lack of intellectual sophistication but the short, tubby and permanently cheerful Heinz could do what Ritter couldn't – he managed to break, shape and transport enough of the volcanic rock to build a house, taking advantage of an overhang on the mountainside that he enclosed with sturdy walls. The result was a residence that one visitor called "uncommonly beautiful."16

The two households now settled down to a strangely distant existence. They were friendly to each other when they met, but took steps to make sure that wasn't often. The Wittmers might have been attracted to Floreana by stories about Ritter and Strauch, but the reality didn't seem to be their taste. Both Heinz and Margret were fairly conventional and they brought their German values – hard work, neatness and efficiency – with them. The predictable result was that they thrived.17 Under the watchful muzzle of Heinz's Mauser, their crops gave them a steady supply of fruit and vegetables. The Mauser, in turn, gave them a steady supply of pork and beef, as well as cured cattle hides to use as rugs and wall hangings. Later they learned to tan leather from the hides, and Heinz turned out to be a talented cobbler; unlike Ritter and Strauch, who suffered from the glassy lava rock in disintegrating shoes and crude wooden clogs, the Wittmers were safe and comfortable in sturdy leather boots. Hakon Mielche, a Danish writer who met all the residents of Floreana in 1932, was impressed by how normal the Wittmers were. He wrote:

> "When Ritter and the Baroness have turned to dust and "Paradise" and "Eden" have sunk into a smoking hell, Wittmer will still be sitting in his cosy little home smoking his pipe. The sun will rise and set, and he will forget to count the days."18

Mielche's words were prophetic. While the families were incompatible they had managed to come to an arrangement that left them both happy enough. That was all about to change with the arrival of the Baroness.

CHAPTER 3

Eloise Wehrborn de Wagner-Bosquet was born in Austria sometime in the 1890s – details are vague. She was the daughter of a senior Austro-Hungarian government official, but during the war had worked as a secretary in Constantinople, capital of Austria-Hungary's Ottoman ally. Left stranded at the end of the war she managed to get a job in a cabaret. Among the customers was a French merchant called Bosquet, and the pair were soon married. The Baroness returned to France with Bosquet and spent several years in Paris society, but it seems that Bosquet's mother may have been unhappy about the marriage. At any rate she started introducing the Baroness to single men, including two young Germans named Robert Philippson and Rudolf Lorenz.19 Before long the Baroness had started an affair with at least Lorenz and probably both of them. She used some of Bosquet's wealth to finance a ladies' outfitters for Lorenz, but it couldn't last for long – Bosquet discovered the affair and filed for divorce, which was probably his mother's intention.

For the second time in her life the Baroness was out of work and stuck. Now she heard of the Ecuadorean government's land offer on Floreana, and immediately decided to establish a high-class resort there. She spoke to the Ecuadorean consul in Paris and arranged for a plot, then looked for funds to pay for the voyage. Her solution as to sell Lorenz's shop; they took the money and the remaining stock – a large collection of silk underwear – and abandoned their creditors, then sailed for the Galápagos.

The party landed on Floreana in the middle of October 1932, and immediately made an impression. Unfortunately it wasn't a very good one. The group arrived at Friedo with Eloise riding a donkey and her male companions, plus the captain of the supply ship they'd arrived on, walking alongside; the new arrivals managed to annoy Ritter and Strauch almost immediately. One of the men grabbed one of Ritter's deck chairs and set it up for her to sit on, without being invited. She then held her hand out to Strauch, as if expecting it to be kissed; Strauch wrote that the Baroness looked annoyed when she shook the proffered hand instead.20 Things kept going downhill. The visitors stayed so long that it began to get dark, and moving cross-country over the rough terrain of the Galápagos is dangerous at night, so they had to be invited to stay. Eloise then disturbed the others by coughing loudly – and, in Strauch's opinion, theatrically – for much of the night. At one point one of her companions woke Strauch and asked her to make tea for the Baroness; Strauch pointed out that the fire was out and there was no way to boil water, but did provide some sacking to use as an extra blanket. Next day the bad omens continued, as Eloise subtly insulted Strauch's cooking at breakfast and then had a fit of jealousy when one of her party complimented Ritter. Finally the newcomers returned to Post Office Bay, where they had set up a temporary residence in the Norwegian house – this was deserted again following the death of Captain Bruun in a boat accident.

Next the Baroness and her entourage visited the Wittmers. Margret wasn't expecting them and was taken aback by the arrival of this small, slim woman with a large mouth, prominent horsey teeth and a cascade of bleached blonde hair. Her surprise quickly turned to anger. Eloise's first words were barked out; "Where's the spring?" Margret pointed it out to her – and Lorenz took off the Baroness's shoes and washed her feet in it. The spring was the only source of drinking water for the Wittmers and Margret was furious that Eloise so casually contaminated it; it would take time for the pool around it to run clean again.

Visits to the Norwegian house over the next few days made it clear that the Baroness was planning on a long stay on the island. The huge pile of gear she'd brought included a large supply of building materials – tons of cement and stacks of corrugated iron. In conversations with her new neighbors she outlined ambitious plans to build a grand resort hotel on Floreana, which would attract wealthy American tourists and turn the island into a new Monte Carlo. She was obviously excited about it, but the existing residents were less happy. A couple of days had made it clear that she was going to be a disruptive influence on Floreana's quiet community.

The situation quickly escalated. The Wittmers reluctantly gave the Baroness's party permission to camp in their orange grove while they started building a house, which meant they had frequent contact with her. It seems that right from the start she was trying to cause tension among the residents; the ship that brought her had also delivered mail for both households, and Eloise had taken possession of it. Now she gave Margret the mail for the Wittmer family, and handed over a bag for Ritter and Strauch. When Margret delivered it Ritter found that it had all been opened and many items were missing. Ritter immediately blamed the Baroness and Heinz Wittmer worried that she had done it to cause a conflict. The Wittmers themselves were the next victims. The ship that had brought the Baroness had also delivered a hundredweight of rice for the Wittmers2 and they'd paid the captain for it; the rice itself had been stored in Post Office Bay until they had a chance to collect it. A few days later Heinz went down the hill to collect the sack and was met by Eloise. She was dressed in riding gear, heavily made up and carrying a whip; more alarmingly there was a heavy Colt revolver holstered on her belt. Rifles were an essential item on Floreana for hunting and protecting crops from feral animals, but with a population that barely reached double figures there was no reason to be carrying a handgun.

The Baroness obviously thought there was. When Heinz said he was there to collect his rice she announced that he would have to buy it from her. He protested that he'd already bought it from the captain, but she refused to hand it over without payment. Infuriated, he told her to move out of his orange grove. She refused, placing her hand on the Colt to emphasize her words.21 This incident left the

---

2 A hundredweight is 112 pounds – 1/20 of an Imperial ton.

Wittmers in no doubt that Eloise was going to shatter the peace of the island.

In fact her behavior quickly sent ripples beyond Floreana and into the whole Galápagos archipelago. Kristian Estampa was a Norwegian fisherman who lived on Santa Cruz, a larger island about 30 miles north of Floreana. As well as fishing he made some money acting as a ferry service around the islands on his boat Falcon. In November one of his friends, a German travel writer named Franke, arrived in the Galápagos and asked to be taken to Floreana. His plan was to stay with either Ritter or the Wittmers and take advantage of the quiet island atmosphere to get some writing done. Unfortunately he wasn't aware of how much things had changed. Estampa, who often hunted wild cattle on Floreana, didn't know either. That set the stage for the Baroness's worst outburst yet.

On November 9, 1932 Estampa moored the Falcon off Floreana and brought Franke ashore on a small raft he used as a tender. They were accompanied by two of Estampa's Indian workers, who were there to help him hunt. Estampa usually stayed in the Norwegian house when he visited Floreana, but this time he encountered the Baroness, her lovers and the Ecuadorean, Valdivieso. There are different accounts of what happened next. The Wittmers claimed that Eloise refused to let Estampa sleep in the house at Post Office Bay, claiming ownership of it, and that the group then went to Friedo where they were also refused accommodation.22 Dore Strauch claims that she and Ritter didn't know Estampa and Franke had arrived until the next evening.23 It seems likely that the Baroness had told Estampa that she owned the island, the Norwegian had laughed in her face and Eloise and her retinue had threatened him with violence. Estampa and Franke returned to the Falcon, but landed again next day and went hunting. They managed to shoot several wild calves, but while they were carrying them back to the beach they were accosted by the Baroness, Philippson and Valdivieso, who accused them of stealing their property. The hunters were threatened with pistols, then Philippson and Valdivieso smashed Estampa's raft, marooning them on the island. The

hunting party scattered under the guns of
Eloise and her sidekicks; Estampa and the Indians fled to Friedo and Franke to the Wittmers's
house. Estampa was injured, perhaps from a
beating or maybe from the hazards of fleeing
through a landscape littered with cactus, thorn
bushes and jagged volcanic rock.

At the Wittmer home Franke begged Heinz
to row the group to the safety of the Falcon.
The Wittmers had brought a collapsible rowing
boat to the island with them; it had been kept
in Post Office Bay since they arrived, but after
the incident with the stolen rice they had begun hiding it in the bush along the shore in
case Eloise's greedy eyes fell on it and she decided to either "sell" it to them or keep it for
herself. In calm weather Heinz knew he could
row Franke to the moored Falcon easily
enough, but right now the sea was rough; it
would be risky. There was also the risk of of-
fending the Baroness by helping people she
had decided to make her enemies. The situation had degenerated into violence, though,
and it was obviously vital to get Estampa and

Franke off Floreana as soon as possible. There
was no alternative – the risk had to be taken.24

Next day Heinz and Harry took Franke
down to the coast and unearthed the collapsible boat. They rowed out to the Falcon and put
Franke on board; the plan was that he would
then tow the collapsible round to Black Beach,
a small anchorage not far from Friedo. The plan
didn't quite work out, however. It was only
once Franke was on board Falcon that it became obvious he had no idea how to handle a
boat. Falcon was a motor sailer, designed as a
yacht, which had been given to Estampa by the
British millionaire Viscount Astor. She wasn't
suitable for novices and Franke couldn't keep
her under control. Heinz decided that the only
solution was to moor Falcon again, leave
Franke on board then row to Black Beach and
collect Estampa from Friedo. He and Harry
made two more perilous trips out to the Falcon, once carrying Estampa and then, after he
had sailed her round to Black Beach, with the
two Indians. Both Margret and Strauch suffered
terrible anxiety knowing that Heinz and Harry
were at sea in the small, fragile collapsible –

the heavily pregnant Margret could hear the crashing surf from her house – and their fears increased as night fell. It was a huge relief when they returned safely home, stopping off at Friedo on the way to let Strauch know they'd survived.

CHAPTER 4

The first problems with the Baroness had been irritating, but the incident with Estampa and Franke left the residents of Floreana seriously alarmed. It was bad enough that Eloise and her group were willing to draw weapons to resolve a trivial issue. What was worse was the way she seemed to be trying to set herself up as the ruler of the island. She had been granted a plot of land by the Ecuadorean government, but so had Ritter and the Wittmers; to suddenly claim that she owned the island and had the right to deny others hunting rights – or to charge what were effectively customs fees on goods landed for others – was both absurd and worrying. Even before Heinz's adventures in the collapsible boat Ritter had decided it was time to inform the Ecuadorean authorities.

Since the collapse of the penal colony decades earlier there had been no official Ecuadorean presence on Floreana, but there was a military garrison on San Cristóbal. This island is the easternmost in the Galápagos, nearly 60 miles from Floreana, and at the time it was the center of government activity in the archipelago. The island's governor was Major Aguilera of the Ecuadorean Army, and he commanded a military garrison consisting of his adjutant and thirteen soldiers, whose main job was to keep a warning light for shipping lit at night.25 They weren't a very impressive force – in fact they were a gaggle of scruffy, badly equipped troops who more often than not failed to light the warning lamp at night – but they were the only government representatives in reach, so Ritter put down his concerns in a letter. He described the Baroness's outrageous behavior and his fears of more serious crimes in the future, and begged the authorities to remove her from the island. The letter was handed to Estampa for delivery to the governor. The problem was that even if Aguilera didn't feel the need to get advice from the mainland first it could take weeks for him to act; the little group of settlers didn't know if they had that long before the Baroness's megalomania led to something even worse.

As it turned out things progressed on a happier note. Margret had been able to do less and less work as her pregnancy progressed, so she was relieved when she felt the first labor pains on December 30. Heinz wanted to go for Ritter, believing that his medical training would be useful, but Margret persuaded him not to. They prepared for the event by boiling water and laying out clean linen, but the pangs subsided. Next day Margret felt better and worked to bake cakes to celebrate the New Year. January 1 wasn't a festive occasion though; the cramps returned and she was left feeling depressed. Finally she went into labor after nightfall, and the baby boy was born around 3 the next morning.26 Ritter was finally summoned to help with the afterbirth, earning Margret's gratitude for his help. Heinz offered to pay Ritter for his assistance but the doctor declined; there was no use for money on the island, he said. He did add that he would appreciate a bag of dried meat every two weeks to feed his chickens. Margret, who was well aware of both Ritter's vegetarian ideals and his frequent failure to stick to them, found that amusing.27

Over the next few days the other residents came to visit Margret and the baby, who was named Rolf – Margret left the decision to Harry. Dore Strauch became very sentimental over the birth but also, in her diary, sadly compared the Germanic neatness of the Wittmer home to the Bohemian clutter and mess of Friedo. Then Lorenz arrived, bringing a cowhide as a gift. He also brought news from "the wigwam," Margret's derogatory name for the ramshackle tent the Baroness's group were living in while they planned the construction of their luxury resort. Valdivieso had quarreled with Philippson and left the group. At first he had planned to work for either Ritter or the Wittmers, then, realizing that was impractical (mainly because he wouldn't be welcome) had moved to Post Office Bay until he could find a ship that would take him back to the mainland. There were also hints of changes in the

relationship among the remains of the entourage. Up to now Lorenz had been firmly in
Eloise's favor as her primary lover, but now he
mentioned that he had to take Valdivieso his
meals every day.28 This seemed like a menial
task for someone Margret had previously
called the Baroness's "constant companion."

A few days later the Baroness herself visited
the Wittmers. Unlike their last encounters she
was all sweetness and light, and announced
that the previous "misunderstandings" had all
been Valdivieso's fault. Now, she was sure,
there would be peace and harmony. Margret
was skeptical but held her tongue. Eloise also
brought a gift - baby clothes for Rolf. She
claimed they came from Lorenz's shop in Paris
but this seems unlikely. It's more probable they
had been sent to Margret by a friend on the
mainland and intercepted by Eloise, who was
now routinely opening all mail left in Post Office Bay.

One result of Rolf's birth was that relations
between Friedo's residents and the Wittmers
became somewhat closer. Margret and
Strauch, particularly, seem to have had long

conversations about island life and, of course, the Wittmer's loathing of the Baroness. Eloise might have talked of a happy, peaceful future, but Margret Wittmer for one didn't believe a word of it.

CHAPTER 5

While Margret was caring for her new baby the Baroness and her two companions were working on their grand resort hotel. Ritter and Strauch visited this structure on their way back from visiting the Wittmers. It was a strange project. The gardens that surrounded it were immaculately laid out – although Friedrich was dismissive of the small vegetable plots – but the "hotel" itself was nothing more than a crude shack. A three foot high log wall formed the foundations, then canvas from a cut-up tent screened the next three feet and a corrugated iron roof perched on the support poles to keep the rain out.29 Eloise told them that it had been built by Valdivieso, who she said was "the only one of the men who understood manual labor."30 Since her arrival she had claimed that Lorenz and Philippson were architects but there's no evidence that this was true; it certainly didn't show in the design of the "Hacienda Paradise." The interior was a surprise though. The rickety walls were lined with Persian rugs and the Baroness reclined on a large sofa decorated with silk cushions.

Strauch had promised Margret that she would try to persuade the Baroness to act more reasonably, so she invited Eloise and her companions to a meal at Friedo. She intended it as a peace offering, a chance to make a new start and put the previous issues behind them. It seems she also wanted to impress Lorenz, because she included some of his favorites on the menu. She was to be disappointed though; the Baroness arrived with Philippson and explained that Lorenz had been suddenly taken ill – a recurrence of tuberculosis he had previously suffered from – and was staying in the house at Post Office Bay. This left Strauch extremely angry. From her account she appears to have taken a liking to Lorenz and now she was concerned about his health. If he was ill, she thought, Ritter should have been summoned to examine and treat him. He also shouldn't be alone in a decrepit building in the damp air of the shore. The meal didn't get off to a good start.

It soon got worse. The Baroness, as usual, had ridden to Friedo on her much-abused donkey. During the meal it began to bray noisily, as donkeys are prone to doing. Strauch left the table and let it in to the corral where she kept her own donkey. Strauch was very attached to this animal, which she had named Burro. Shortly afterwards she realized she'd forgotten to give the donkeys fresh water and went out again to fill the trough. Eloise seemed irritated at this; the conversation consisted of a seemingly endless monologue about her talents, achievements and amazing popularity, and having part of her audience periodically going out to look after donkeys didn't please her. When Strauch left the table a third time in response to Burro's call she snapped; "If you treat your husband as well as you do your donkey, what a happy man he must be!" This, combined with a stream of sexually suggestive remarks to Ritter and revelations of sadistic hunting trips around the island, plunged Strauch's opinion of the

Baroness to a new low. It would soon fall lower still.

Captain G. Allan Hancock was an American oil millionaire and philanthropist with a deep personal interest in science. As well as running the Rancho La Brea Oil Company and support-ing a number of causes in Southern California he spent years travelling the world, often in the company of renowned scientists, investigating anything that caught his interest. For these trips he had a motor yacht, the Velera III, built; as well as being extremely luxurious she was also fully equipped for scientific research. On January 28, 1933 he landed on Floreana with a group of scientists, including Professor Waldo L. Schmidt from the Washington Museum.31 Hancock had read about Ritter and Strauch and was eager to meet them; he had also brought gifts of tools, medical supplies, and small luxu-ries for all the settlers. His group – which in-cluded several German speakers – visited the Ritters, where they delivered a large quantity of clothing and tools. They then visited the Wittmers, where they were impressed at how well the family had established themselves in six months, and finally the Hacienda Paradise. Their opinions of that establishment are not recorded.

On February 4 the Baroness and her companions were walking down to the coast with Hancock and his group when, passing Friedo, Eloise saw the pile of gifts that Hancock had given to Ritter. This seems to have sparked her jealousy and possessiveness, because the next day one of them – probably Philippson, going by what came later – went to Friedo and demanded that Ritter shared what he had been given with the Baroness. Ritter understandably refused, leading to an argument. The new era of peace and harmony predicted by Eloise after Rolf's birth was over before it had properly begun.

On February 7 Heinz walked down to Post Office Bay to do some fishing. When he went to get his collapsible boat from its hiding place he discovered it was gone; investigation showed that a roll of wire mesh stored in the old house was also missing. Making his way to Friedo he asked Ritter if he had seen a ship in the bay; perhaps the sailors had found the boat and taken it. Ritter replied that, no, there had been no ship. That narrowed the list of suspects dramatically and left Heinz furious.

Although the grand hotel was simply a crude shack the Baroness had placed a large sign in Post Office Bay inviting guests to visit. It was a dramatic and poetic promise of tropical luxury, although the effect was slightly spoiled by it being handwritten in pencil.32 Eloise was determined to realize her vision of a luxury hotel attracting the world's richest and most prominent travelers, even if that determination didn't extend to actually building a hotel. On March 16 a potential guest dropped anchor in the bay – another member of the prominent Astor family, New York millionaire Vincent Astor. Philippson made his way down to the shore and found a boat, which belonged to another visitor to the island. He took the boat without asking permission and rowed out to Astor's yacht, where he delivered a handwritten invitation to the Hacienda. Astor read the invitation, shook his head and handed it back.

Infuriated, Philippson made his way up to Friedo and confronted Ritter. He accused the doctor of slandering the Baroness and her group, deterring visitors from going to the Hacienda. If it happened again, he warned, he would give Ritter a beating. That threat proved to be unwise. Philippson was tall and powerfully built,33 whereas Ritter was short and thin; the young man must have thought he could easily intimidate his intended victim. Ritter turned out to be stronger than he looked, however. More specifically he was strong enough to grab Philippson, drag him to the gate and throw him bodily out of Friedo.

Within days Philippson repeated his tactics with the Wittmers. A sick donkey had gone missing from the Hacienda and the Baroness had got it into her head that the Wittmers were hiding it. Philippson turned up at their house and demanded they return it. When they denied it was there he became abusive until finally Heinz too lost his temper. Philippson was ejected from that house too, and in the future steered clear of the family.

On May 17 an Indian appeared at the Wittmer home and asked them to collect mail from the Hacienda. Arriving there Margret found

that the crew of the ship San Cristóbal had
brought a shipment they had sent from Germany before their departure as well as a sack
of mail. Margret was delighted, and also curi-
ous to see that Major Aguilero had arrived as
well. He wanted to speak to the Baroness
about Ritter's letter of complaint but she had
disappeared along with Philippson. Dedicated
as ever the Major left with the crew of the ship,
his mission incomplete.

Among the sack of mail were some German
newspapers, which the Wittmers shared with
Ritter and Strauch. They were astonished to
find lurid stories about life on the island, which
Ritter decided were Franke's revenge on the
Baroness for his treatment of her. According to
reports she had declared herself empress of
Floreana and was surrounded by a "terror regi-
ment" of twelve freebooters, who had captured Ritter and led him away in chains.
Margret was upset by the stories but Ritter
found them amusing. So did Eloise, although
for a different reason – she was charmed by the
idea that someone had labeled her an empress.

The Major returned on May 30 and this time he succeeded in catching the Baroness at home. His investigation into the conflict on Floreana was a short one though; it lasted barely 24 hours, at the end of which Eloise was told that her territory covered four square kilometers (about 1.5 square miles). The Major probably hoped that setting a clear limit to her property would discourage her from acting so imperiously on the rest of the island. He overlooked her capacity to terrorize those who shared it with her.

CHAPTER 6

Nobody knows how much pirates stole during the so-called Golden Age of Piracy from about 1650 to 1730 and the sporadic outbreaks of sea robbery that lasted into the 19th century, but it must have added up to many billions of dollars at today's values. We do know, pretty well, what they did with it. Some pirate captains saved and invested their loot and used it to break into legitimate trade after disbanding their crews and putting away the black flag. Most squandered it on rum and women. The one thing they almost never did is what they're most famous for – bury it on a deserted island, and record the location on a chart marked with skeletons and cryptic clues. The reality is that anyone looking for a hoard of buried pirate gold is more or less guaranteed disappointment.

Reality, of course, never figured very highly in Eloise's plans. Her group began to spend the evenings digging by lantern light in an attempt to locate buried treasure. The residents of the Hacienda had now expanded again; a Dane, Knud Arends, had been employed by the Baroness.34 Arends had worked for Major Aguilera as an interpreter but hadn't had a permanent job in quite a while, so he was happy to accept the offer or a regular income. It's likely he wasn't so keen on being dragged into mad schemes like scrabbling in the lava rubble looking for an old sea chest full of pieces of eight that wasn't actually there but he was quickly learning about the Baroness's eccentricities. It didn't take long before he fell victim to them.

In early October there were more visitors to the island. Werner Boeckmann, a German journalist who'd been there a few weeks ago and had promised to bring the Wittmers copies of some photos he'd taken, had brought his brother in law Herr Linde with him and the Baroness invited them on a hunting trip. A group of the Major's soldiers also joined the expedition. Safe hunting needs organization and

discipline to make sure lines of fire are clear,
but that didn't happen here. Both the Baroness
and one of the soldiers fired at the same time;
both missed their targets but one of the bullets
hit Arends in the stomach. Although the shot
was fired at close range the bullet remained in
the Dane's body. The Ecuadorean army was
equipped with German Mauser rifles in 7.65mm
Argentine caliber, a high-powered military
round similar to the US .30-06. If the bullet had
come from the soldier it would probably have
passed right through Arends, so most likely the
Baroness's Colt revolver was to blame. Either
way Arends was gravely wounded but not
dead. As he lay screaming on the ground
Boeckmann and Linde, realizing that quick action was needed, ran to Friedo to fetch Ritter.
Returning with them the doctor was able to
stabilize Arends but he needed urgent evacua-
tion to a hospital to extract the bullet. For
three days he was cared for on a makeshift bed
where he had been shot – it was too dangerous
to move him unnecessarily – until the San Cristóbal returned. Philippson went with him to San
Cristóbal Island to see that he was sent on to

Guayaquil on the mainland. To thank Ritter for his help Eloise and Lorenz brought a donkey load of vegetables to Freido; Ritter, disgusted at the pair, refused to accept them.

CHAPTER 7

Relations between the settlers were now at a lower point than ever before. The Wittmers were getting along better with Ritter and Strauch, but between both households and the Baroness mutual loathing was close to the surface and starting to bubble over. Incidents became more serious. Strauch's beloved donkey, Burro, disappeared in summer 1933; months later Ritter caught Lorenz leading it, worn out and exhausted, with a heavy load on its back.

There were wild donkeys roaming Floreana, the descendants of animals let loose by pirates and earlier settlers, and they were a persistent menace to crops. None of the residents had the skills needed to break and train them but the Wittmers had made a useful discovery – donkey flesh is extremely tasty, closely resembling venison. Whenever one of them tried to raid the garden after that Heinz loaded his trusty Mauser and for the next few days donkey was on the menu. One night in November they were woken by the distinctive braying sound from their garden and Heinz went out with the rifle. Sure enough a donkey was busily eating its way along a row of vegetables. He worked the bolt, aimed and fired, dropping it cleanly – but when he examined the carcass he recognized it as Burro, who should have been securely corralled at Friedo. Even worse, when he checked the barbed wire fence that surrounded the garden it was unbroken; the donkey hadn't entered through one of the gaps the wild bulls occasionally tore in the wire. Instead the gate stood open. Its latch could only have been unfastened by human hands – someone had deliberately led the donkey into the garden. Everyone on the island was well aware of Heinz's direct approach to marauding animals so it was clear someone had planned to have Burro shot – and it was very unlikely to have been Ritter or Strauch.

Knowing how upset Strauch would be if she found out what had happened the Wittmers, torn with guilt, buried Burro. Two days later Lorenz turned up at their home and asked them not to shoot at donkeys as several of theirs had escaped. He claimed that someone had turned them loose during the night. Heinz gave him a skeptical stare; Lorenz couldn't look him in the eyes. Later Heinz decided to check on the Baroness's donkeys and found them all on a nearby meadow, securely tied.

Next beans and papayas started vanishing from the Wittmer garden. It was obvious the thief wasn't an animal – there were no tracks in the dirt, and besides the fence remained unbroken. After a few days they found human footprints, and then one morning Margret saw Philippson leaving the garden at around 5am. There was no point complaining to the Baroness though. Instead Heinz, with advice from Ritter, wrote a letter to the governor questioning Eloise's mental health and asking for stronger action against her.

The Wittmers were having a few doubts about the mental health of Ritter and Strauch, too. There had been periods of tension between the two ever since they had arrived on the island, but things now seemed to be deteriorating. Strauch made no secret of the fact that Ritter often beat her, and in fact almost seemed to be boasting of it. Justifying his actions with pseudo-Nietzschean philosophy she claimed that a woman should always be completely submissive to a man. It would be inaccurate to call the Wittmer marriage one of equals – they were very conventional Germans of their time – but they were uncomfortable with these masochistic ravings and, while they sympathized with Strauch, her domestic situation kept a distance between the two households. That was unfortunate, because now was when they most needed to present a united front to their common enemy.

Relations were also breaking down inside the Hacienda. When the Baroness had first arrived Lorenz had been the more favored of her two lovers, but at some point that began to change. Gradually she transferred her affections to Philippson and Lorenz was increasingly given menial and exhausting jobs to do. As time passed he got into the habit of visiting Friedo and pouring out his troubles to Dore Strauch, who was always happy to lend a sympathetic ear. With the arrival of Arends things changed again; the Dane was Eloise's favorite during the day, but at night she went to bed with Philippson. Lorenz remained in the role of abused servant. Nevertheless Philippson was insanely jealous of Arends and became increasingly prone to violent rages. Finally, in mid-March 1934, he blew up at Lorenz and beat him so badly that he was unconscious for several hours. When he came around again he couldn't face returning to the Hacienda; instead he ran away to Friedo, where he hoped Strauch's sympathy would earn him a refuge. It might well have done that but Ritter was less forgiving of past events and turned the battered man firmly away. They would give him enough bananas to keep him alive, Ritter said, but that was all; he wasn't welcome to stay with them.

That left only one option left – the Wittmers. When Lorenz turned up they, too, realized there was no alternative. He couldn't return to Eloise and Philippson, and Ritter wouldn't take him in. He would have to stay with the Wittmers until the San Cristóbal's next visit. Lorenz had had enough of life in the island – he wanted to return to Germany. That suited Heinz and Margret just fine because the sooner the strange, brooding young man was out of their home the happier they would be.

Before the ship could return to collect Lorenz, however, something happened on Floreana. It's impossible to say exactly what it was because the surviving inhabitants swept it under a cloak of silence and, almost certainly, lies. It's not hard to piece the rough outline together, though. After six months of deteriorating relations and spiteful pranks, murder came to the island.

CHAPTER 8

The main source for what happened next is Margret Wittmer. According to her, on March 27, 1934 Lorenz, wanting to repay the Wittmers for hosting him by helping with chores, went with Heinz to collect wood. While they were gone Eloise came to the gate and asked to speak to Lorenz. When Margret told her that he was out she left a message for him; some friends had arrived on a yacht and were going to take her and Philippson on a cruise to the South Seas. Lorenz was to look after the house and the animals until she sent him a message. Unsurprisingly Margret said she was overjoyed at the news;

> *"I can hardly believe my ears! The thing that we have longed for is to become a reality."*

At dinner that night she passed on the good news to Heinz and Lorenz. They were skeptical, she says, and after they had eaten Lorenz went to the Hacienda to see if the Baroness and Philippson were still there. The shack was deserted. To make sure he then walked to Post Office Bay. The old Norwegian house was also empty but there were footprints on the beach. The next day Lorenz moved back into the Hacienda, then went to tell Ritter and Strauch what had happened. They danced with joy, Margret reported.35

Margret's account is a joyful one; a happy ending to the tension, strife and violence that the Baroness and her entourage had brought to Floreana. There's only one problem with it.

It almost certainly isn't true.

There were certainly plenty of yachts passing through the islands and many of them visited Floreana – the wild tales of events on the island, and of the Baroness's strange existence in a rickety shack hung with silk and exotic carpets had spread far and wide – but nobody saw one anchor there on March 27, 1934. Friedrich

Ritter, who had a view of the best anchorages from the house at Friedo, was particularly adamant that he hadn't seen any vessel around that time. In fact both he and Strauch wrote that they were highly skeptical of the Wittmer's tale and they had some evidence to back up their skepticism.

Ritter admitted that with Eloise and Philippson gone he had urged Lorenz to sell what he could from the Hacienda and use the money to return to Germany. He had an ulterior motive, of course; unlike the Wittmers he had reserves of cash, and intended to buy as much as he could himself. He did notice that both Lorenz and the Wittmers were utterly convinced that the Baroness would never return. He also noticed that they seemed to have taken remarkably little with them when they left, which was strange if – as Margret claimed – she had planned to restart her hotel scheme on Tahiti, which she believed would attract more millionaire yachtsmen. Ritter's suspicions turned to near certainty when he found a small book discarded on the floor of the decrepit house.

The Picture of Dorian Grey is one of Oscar Wilde's best-known novels. It describes a young society man's descent into depravity, and something in the story appealed strongly to Eloise Bosquet-Wagner. That isn't really surprising, as she was something of an expert in corrupting young men. Anyway, she brought a copy of the novel to Floreana with her and re-read in endlessly. When she entertained guests in her ramshackle paradise she usually reclined on one of her sofas in a favorite outfit – either riding gear or French silk underwear were her go-to choices – with the book clasped in one hand.36 The book was her constant companion and except when she was away from the Hacienda, hunting or just prowling her self-proclaimed empire, it almost never left her side. Now, standing among the ruins of her domain, Ritter turned the little volume thoughtfully in his hands. Would she have left such a treasured possession behind when she left Floreana, perhaps forever? He didn't think so.

So what really happened to the Baroness and her remaining lover? It's unlikely that so colorful character could have left the

Galápagos and never been heard from again, and no yacht was reported missing in the Pacific that might have picked her up from Floreana. It's almost certain that one of the enemies she'd worked so hard to create had finally had enough of her. Far from civilization, with no law enforcement closer that San Cristóbal, the temptation to act as judge, jury and double executioner must have been strong – especially after Major Aguilera's ineffectual attempt at restoring the peace. No trace of Eloise or Philippson was ever found but that's no great mystery. It's been speculated that the killer could have disposed of their victims with a pyre of acacia wood, which is plentiful on the island and burns hot enough to disintegrate bone. That would have worked, but an even easier solution would have been to simply throw the bodies to the sharks.

Who is likely to have committed the killings? The one with the strongest motive was certainly Rudolf Lorenz. Abandoned and exploited by the Baroness, and viciously abused by Philippson, it's easy to see him snapping. Could he have killed his tormentors, though? By

March 1934 he was a very sick man, far weaker than Philippson, and he had been weakened even more by poor diet and constant hard work. The Baroness was small and slender but almost always armed. Lorenz had the motive, but he probably didn't have the ability.

Who does that leave? Friedrich Ritter and Dore Strauch certainly disliked the denizens of the Hacienda, but they had kept themselves neutral as much as possible. Margret Wittmer was even less capable of overpowering Eloise and Philippson than Lorenz was, and the same applies to Harry – his health had improved greatly since coming to Floreana, but his eyesight was very bad and he was only 14 years old.

That leaves Heinz Wittmer – the amiable, practical and devoted family man who along with his wife was, all accounts make clear, the most sensible resident of the island. Heinz was unfailingly pleasant and good natured, and possessed of the rock-solid conventional outlook of a middle class German. Even in this hard, forbidding tropical environment he had managed to build a lifestyle that reflected sensible German values as closely as he could manage. He was probably frustrated by the failure of the islands' governor to control the situation on Floreana, though, and to a German the most important of social values is that "alles in ordnung" – everything is in order. Eloise Bosquet-Wagner gloried in disorder and spread it wherever she went. As her behavior became increasingly erratic the mild-mannered Heinz must have been extremely worried. He lived only a few hundred yards from an unpredictable armed madwoman and her aggressive lover; it was an ever-present threat to his family and the sanctuary they had created. Heinz had proven many times that he could act decisively if his crops were threatened. When the violence bubbling inside the Hacienda Paradise began to spill out across the island did he give a resigned sigh, thumb a clip into the magazine of his Mauser, chamber a round and slip out into the night?

We'll probably never know.

THE AFTERMATH

After the Baroness and Philippson vanished life on Floreana slowly returned to an even keel, but there was a further wave of tragedy to come. Lorenz lived in the house at Post Office Bay for months, waiting in vain for a ship to take him away. He was in a deep depression and his health continued to deteriorate; Margret Wittmer was convinced he was dying. In the end he was picked up by Trygve Nuggerud, a Norwegian who lived on Santa Cruz Island. That made three people on board Nuggerud's motor yacht Dinamita; a twelve-year-old Ecuadorean cabin boy, Lorenz and Nuggerud himself. They left Floreana on July 11, reached Santa Cruz the next day and set out for San Cristóbal from where Lorenz planned to catch a ship to the mainland. They never arrived.

On November 17 an American tuna boat passing Marchena Island spotted something suspicious on shore and sent a landing party to investigate. On the beach they found a small sailing skiff that had come from Nuggerud's yacht with the Norwegian's mummified body sprawled beside it. A few yards further up the beach was the leathery corpse of Lorenz. The mutilated remains of a seal lay close by; the two men had killed it, then eaten part of it raw – spent matches and a pile of wood and burned paper showed where they had tried, and failed, to light a fire. They had also slit its throat with a razor blade and drunk its blood, in a desperate attempt to slake their thirst. There was no fresh water near their landing site; they had both died of dehydration.

Marchena Island lies over 50 miles to the north of Santa Cruz; to reach San Cristóbal they should have been heading east. Dinamita was an old boat, a motor yacht with no sailing rig, and the most likely answer to the mystery is that her engine failed. With no power she would have been swept north by the currents that run through the islands. Knowing that

Marchena was at the northern edge of the Galápagos, and that a thousand miles of open ocean lay between there and the coast of Guatemala, Nuggerud and Lorenz must have made the decision to strike out for shore in the tiny skiff. Perhaps the cabin boy, Jose Pasmino, refused to leave the illusory safety of the Dinamita. No trace of either was ever found and their remains probably lie far to the north of the islands, four miles under the surface of the Pacific.

Just days after Captain Borthen of the tuna boat found the corpses on Marchena another drama was played out to the end back on Floreana. On November 20 Strauch, tired and hysterical, stumbled in the door of the Wittmer's house. She told Margret that Ritter was ill, and perhaps dying, after eating some home-canned chicken. Margret found some rubber tubing to use as a stomach pump and hurried down to Friedo, questioning Strauch on the way. Both of them, Strauch said, had eaten the potted chicken the day before. She had immediately vomited; Ritter had not, but had become ill later. Strauch was vague about why she had waited so long to come for help and Margret, who knew that the pair had often argued violently, was suspicious. Still, she was unprepared for Ritter's condition. It was clearly too late for a stomach pump to help him; he was dying, probably of botulism poisoning. Still he lingered, conscious but unable to speak. Heinz joined them in the early evening around the time Ritter picked up a pencil and, glaring at Strauch, scrawled his last message – "I curse you with my dying breath." Then he collapsed back onto his bed. He died in the night, leaving Strauch hysterical. Next day Heinz and Harry buried him in the garden at Friedo. Strauch stayed away from the simple ceremony.

Captain Allan Hancock, who had been told by letter about the disappearance of Eloise and Philippson, returned to Floreana on December 4. Hancock immediately began signaling to Friedo by flashing a mirror, but there was no reply. Margret and Strauch, seeing the big white yacht moored in the bay, walked down to the shore to meet the explorer. There they passed on the news of the deaths of Lorenz, Nuggerud and Ritter. Strauch also told John

Garth, one of Hancock's scientists, that Ritter had been "very abusive" to her in the days before his death – exactly the opposite of what she later wrote.

Dore Strauch left Floreana forever on December 7, aboard the Velero III. She was just ahead of a swarm of journalists who flocked to the island, alerted by a radio message about Ritter's death sent by Hancock to the Ecuadorean authorities. The world's media enjoyed one last frenzy of reporting on the strange events of the last year, and then Floreana sank back into obscurity. Seven adults had come to the island in 1932 and 1933; now two were dead in mysterious circumstances, two more had vanished from the face of the Earth and a fifth was heading back to Germany, a strange and tattered figure on one of the world's most luxurious yachts. The story had everything a journalist could wish for.

But of those seven adults two remained. Heinz and Margret went on to prosper when the Galápagos became a tourist destination after the Second World War. Their descendants, wealthy now, still own property and businesses on Floreana. Hakon Mielche's words, written before farce turned to tragedy, had been prophetic; Ritter and the Baroness had turned to dust but Heinz Wittmer, with his wife, his children and his Mauser rifle, was still sitting in his cozy little house smoking his pipe.

READY FOR MORE?

We hope you enjoyed reading this series. If you are ready to read similar stories, check out other books in the *Cold Case Crimes* series:

Jeff Davis 8: The True Story Behind the Unsolved Murder That Allegedly Inspired True Detective, Season One (By Fergus Mason)

Jefferson Davis Parish has been described as quaint, and in many ways it certainly is. For anyone from a big city much of the area, especially out among the farms, is like a trip in a time machine. For a sleepy rural community, however, Jefferson Davis is a lot more violent than you'd expect, and these days cheap, potent rocks of cocaine are at the root of a lot of that violence.

Crack addicts are famously willing to do just about anything to subsidize their habit so street prostitution has become a real issue, mostly concentrated in the town's poorer neighborhoods south of the railway track. Prostitution – especially on the street – is a dangerous business, so the sheriff's office weren't too surprised when the first one turned up dead. As the body count climbed people started to take notice, but despite all their efforts the killings continued until eight women were dead.

This book traces one of the most fascinating unsolved crimes in the history of Louisiana. In 2014, many believe it became one of the inspirations for the first season of HBO's "True Detective." But the crimes in this book are much more shocking than anything captured on TV.

The Martyr of El Salvador: The Assassination of Óscar Romero (By Reagan Martin)

Óscar Romero, a respected Catholic priest, called on soldiers, as Christians, to put down their arms and stop carrying out the governments order to strip citizens of the most basic human rights...for this he was assassinated. For over 30 years, his murder has gone unsolved.

Who would murder a priest who only wanted to stop the injustice? And more importantly, why is it that, with substantial evidence naming the murderers involved, was nothing done to convict those guilty of murdering the country's beloved archbishop?

Annihilation In Austin: The Servant Girl Annihilator Murders of 1885 (By Tim Huddleston)

Murder. Chaos. Outrage. This was the mode in Texas' capital city, Austin from 1884 to 1885. The city had been haunted by a string of bloody murders. Women were not just killed-- they were dragged alive from their beds, taken outside where they were often tortured and then murdered. Six of the victims, all women, were found dead with sharp objects inserted in their ears.

As horrifying as the murders were, what's more horrifying is that the person who committed these heinous acts of violence was never found. To this day it remains one of the most famous unsolved crimes. It has long been suspected by several noted historians that the real killer may have been none other than Jack the Ripper.

Written with gripping, page turning suspense, this book brings you back in time to Austin, Texas, so you can experience the horror and panic for yourself. Faint at heart turn away!

The Axeman: The Brutal History of the Axeman of New Orleans (By Wallace Edwards)

Between 1918 to 1919 a serial killer ran rampant throughout New Orleans. His weapon of choice? The axe. He didn't spare women. Or children. Or even men. There was only one kind of person who could be sparred from the blade of his axe: the home of a person playing jazz music. At least eight people were brutally murdered. Who could have been responsible for this crime, and how was the Mafia connected? Did a corrupt police department intentionally leave this case unsolved?

Come, if you dare, as Absolute Crime takes you

on the hunt for one of the most brutal killers who ever lived.

Young, Queer, and Dead: A Biography of San Francisco's Most Overlooked Serial Killer, The Doodler (By Reagan Martin)

The Zodiac Killer may have been San Francisco's most notorious serial killer, but another equally cruel killer was also stalking the streets at the same time, and, just like the Zodiac Killer, has never been arrested for his crimes. The difference is, while the Zodiac Killer's murder spree was heavily publicized, this other killer, nicknamed The Doodler, went unreported by the media and is nearly unknown today.

How did this ruthless killer become almost forgotten? Because he didn't target helpless women or children--he targeted gays--and in the 70s many people believed they had it coming; if they would just stop being gay, then all would be well.

In this gripping short book, you will go on the trail for one of the most brutal killers who ever lived. Read about why his victims were disregarded by a homophobic press, and how he was positively identified by three escaped victims...only to walk away free without being arrested.

Getting Away With Murder: 15 Chilling Cold Cases That Will Make You Think Twice About Going Outside (By William Webb)

Despite a decline in the number of murders in the United States since the 1960s, thousands go unsolved each year. As of 2013, the solve rate was at an all time low at only 65 percent of the total committed.

The 15 murders profiled in this book were committed between 1958 and 2014. The oldest of the set involves the bizarre murder of Pearl Eaton, one of the famous Ziegfeld Follies Girls of the 1920s. From the beginning, the crime had no leads or suspects and remains among the coldest of the 15 unsolved crimes. The most recent – the murder of four members of the McStay family found buried in the California desert in November 2013 – is under active investigation.

Newsletter Offer

Don't forget to sign up for your newsletter to grab your free book:

http://www.absolutecrime.com/newsletter

NOTES

[1] Treherne, John; *The Galapagos Affair*

[2] Badische Seiten, *Freiburg in Großherzogtum Baden (1805—1918)*
http://www.badische-seiten.de/freiburg/geschichte-grossherzogtum-baden.php

[3] Treherne, John; *The Galapagos Affair*

[4] Strauch, Dore, *Satan Came to Paradise*

[5] Smithsonian Institution, *The Empress of the Galapagos Islands, Part 2*
http://siarchives.si.edu/blog/empress-galapagos-islands-part-2

[6] Frommers, *Galapagos Islands – In Depth*
http://www.frommers.com/destinations/galapagos-islands/672372

[7] Badische Zeitung, Jan 17, 2009, *Nach dem Partnertausch ins Paradies*
http://www.badische-zeitung.de/kandern/nach-dem-partnertausch-ins-paradies--10401124.html

[8] Treherne, John; *The Galapagos Affair*

[9] Strauch, Dore, *Satan Came to Paradise*

[10] Cousteau, Jacques-Yves & Cousteau, Philippe, *The Shark: Splendid Savage of the Sea*

[11] Treherne, John; *The Galapagos Affair*

[12] Strauch, Dore, *Satan Came to Paradise*

[13] Treherne, John; *The Galapagos Affair*

[14] BBC History, *Konrad Adenauer (1876-1967)*

http://www.bbc.co.uk/history/historic_figures/adenauer_konrad.shtml

[15] Treherne, John; *The Galapagos Affair*

[16] Mielche, Hakon, *Let's See if the World is Round*

http://www.galapagos.to/TEXTS/MIELCHE.HTM

[17] Smithsonian Institution, *The Empress of the Galapagos Islands, Part 3*
http://siarchives.si.edu/blog/empress-galapagos-islands-part-3

[18] Mielche, Hakon, *Let's See if the World is Round*
http://www.galapagos.to/TEXTS/MIELCHE.HTM

[19] Smithsonian Institution, *The Empress of the Galapagos Islands, Part 2*
http://siarchives.si.edu/blog/empress-galapagos-islands-part-2

[20] Strauch, Dore, *Satan Came to Paradise*

[21] Stern, Mar 24, 2008, *Die Kaiserin von Galapagos*
http://www.stern.de/panorama/floreana-die-kaiserin-von-galapagos-614377.html

[22] Wittmer, Margret, *What Happened on Galapagos*
http://www.galapagos.to/TEXTS/WITTMER1.PHP

[23] Treherne, John; *The Galapagos Affair*

[24] Wittmer, Margret, *What Happened on Galapagos*
http://www.galapagos.to/TEXTS/WITTMER1.PHP

[25] Mielche, Hakon, *Let's See if the World is Round*
http://www.galapagos.to/TEXTS/MIELCHE.HTM

[26] Wittmer, Margret, *What Happened on Galapagos*
http://www.galapagos.to/TEXTS/WITTMER1.PHP

[27] Treherne, John; *The Galapagos Affair*

[28] Wittmer, Margret, *What Happened on Galapagos*
http://www.galapagos.to/TEXTS/WITTMER1.PHP

[29] Wittmer, Margret, *What Happened on Galapagos*
http://www.galapagos.to/TEXTS/WITTMER1.PHP

[30] Treherne, John; *The Galapagos Affair*

[31] Wittmer, Margret, *What Happened on Galapagos*
http://www.galapagos.to/TEXTS/WITTMER1.PHP

[32] Mielche, Hakon, *Let's See if the World is Round*

http://www.galapagos.to/TEXTS/MIELCHE.HTM

[33] Mielche, Hakon, *Let's See if the World is Round*
http://www.galapagos.to/TEXTS/MIELCHE.HTM

[34] Wittmer, Margret, *What Happened on Galapagos*
http://www.galapagos.to/TEXTS/WITTMER1.PHP

[35] Wittmer, Margret, *What Happened on Galapagos*
http://www.galapagos.to/TEXTS/WITTMER1.PHP

[36] Treherne, John; *The Galapagos Affair*

www.ingramcontent.com/pod-product-compliance
Lightning Source LLC
Chambersburg PA
CBHW051028030426
42336CB00015B/2768